THE DREAM OF K.G.F

THE UNTOLD STORY

KAVEEN SIVA

Contents

CHAPTER ONE

THE WONDER OF MAN CONQUERING THE NATURE

No fairy-tale this! Kolar Gold Field—known through out the globe over just as 'K.G.F' was a pride of India for it was one of the big sources of Gold from which the world benefited since ancient times. Activities for gold extraction commenced on this field since the time man started using this most glittering metal. K.G.F is the richest of all the major and minor Indian Goldfields that brought India the title 'The Golden Peninsula'! Where'er you walk on this field, just pause a while,—be

proud you are standing on the Golden soil! Collect the mud below and around your feet, pan it with water in a vessel,—you get fine powder of gold! K.G.F was the oldest and largest Goldmining industry in India. It has produced more than 800 tonnes of gold through organized modern underground mining from 1880 to 1956 and continued its operations till 2001 for further production. We do not have the actual record, as to the quantum of gold produced from this field during ancient times. It is believed that nearly all the gold referred to in the ancient literature of India was extracted from K.G.F! During 1970s, this mine was producing 100000 ounces of gold every year worth about 3.6 million dollars at the then prevailing rates. At one stage, there was a peak production of 350000 ounces a year! K.G.F contributed 2% of the total gold production of the world which was almost the entire Indian output. It was due to this field India was taken on 'The Gold Map' of the world. As on 2001, the deepest point man penetrated and reached into the planet earth is in K.G.F. The miners here also has driven an

awesome tunnel-working in the undergrounds measuring a total length of 1360 kms within its geographical limits! This mine was the only single largest industry in the world which had a long and unbroken production in history with a peak employ of 35000 workers! Hence, K.G.F in itself is history and the history of it shall amply be called 'The History of a History'. There is no myth or imaginary stories associated with the origin of modern K.G.F because, this is a young city compared with many of the villages surrounding it. But, one will be amazed if they know about the ancient history of K.G.F,—a document you are going to pass through; the first and the only attempt of its kind! Started on a discarded virgin land of 23 sq.miles, the commencement of modern mining here in 1875 expanded into a world famous Goldmine industry. Also, born and grown with it was the Grand Township of Kolar Gold Fields that earned the title 'The Little England'. K.G.F was one of the three largest cities of the erstwhile state of Mysore (Karnataka) with a total population exceeding a lakh in 1940s.

Probably, this must be the only city in India the name of which is called in English abbreviations. K.G.F was so famous and a known name throughout the world. "Bangalore is a city near K.G.F,"—this was how the world countries once referred to the location of the Garden City which is situated at a distance of 90 kms from the Golden City by road! In fact, K.G.F was a child of Bangalore, for it was the British military officers at Bangalore who commenced the Goldmining on this field that resulted in the cre- ation of this town. In the older Atlas of the world, the name of a town Maarikup- pam or Mysore mine finds a place, since it's the starting point of this city. During the earlier days, Maarikuppam Railway station was also called the 'Mysore Mine Terminus'. Of the 39 mining companies floated on this field which included the British, Australian and German companies, the only five joint stock companies of England that established their position as successful miners were:

1. The Mysore Goldmining Company of the firm of M/ s. John Taylor & sons,
2. The Champion reef Goldmining Company of India Limited,
3. The Oorgaum Goldmining Company of India Limited,
4. The Nundydroog Goldmining Company and
5. The Balaghat Goldmining Company Limited.

The famous five lights on the tall mast at Oorgaum was designed to indicate the success of these five established mines of K.G.F! Because of the hard nature of rocks, their high inherent stress (Both vertical and horizontal pressures) and Thermal Gradient (Rising of heat with increase in depths), the gold deposits at deeper levels at K.G.F were the most difficult ones in the world for mining. The successful challenging by men, of many natural problems made K.G.F a world famous centre of hard-rock underground mining. K.G.F mine was a cradle of highly economic activities around K.G.F town. During the time of the British, K.G.F mines were contributing 50% of Karnataka's annual budget. The royalties so derived were invested in many capital ventures of the state thus, generating employment elsewhere in Karnataka. Before planning the annual budgets, the Dewans of the erstwhile Mysore state ascertained from M/s. John Taylor & Sons, the quantum of revenues that might be sent to the government in any year, thus enabling the authorities plan accordingly. K.G.F mines had many a 'firsts' at its credit until 1956. It always stood in tune with the most advanced and sophisticated technical innovations of the world! This was the place where man tried to overwhelm nature; and in return, the astonished nature rewarded men suitably! These men with the Science and Art of modern min- ing and with the state-of—the-art of the days have all achieved glory to the crown

of their motherland. But, this reward,—the enormous gold so produced promoted the luxury of the world, but not the families of workers who extracted it. Surprisingly, the British mining management, the government of erstwhile Mysore state, the British India government and the free India governments all turned their deaf ears and blind eyes to the worst labour condition of the mine workers. The British mine management also succeeded in keeping the outside world in dark about the actual condition prevailed here. Shedding light on these uncertainties by exposing the facts about the fame and fate of this land and its citi- zens to see for yourselves what K.G.F is, is "The History of K.G.F"

CHAPTER TWO

THE LOCATION

Geographically, the mining-land of K.G.F is around 15 kms long to the north-south and 5 kms wide east-west is located in the south-eastern border of the state of Karnataka. This region is a highly mineralized part and is located at the periphery of

Kolar district. The location of this area was once referred to as 5 miles north of Yer- rakonda hill which is 400 ft high (3357 ft above sea-level) and south of Dodduru or Bettarayan hill (2999 ft above sea-level). On top of both these hills are temples in which the presiding deity is Lord Bettarayaswamy. Also, this area lies 9 miles to the east of Budikote. The western border is marked by a large quartzite ridge or the Ulagamadhi dyke also called Doddabetta which is 61 mtrs high (3195 ft above sea- level). To its south-east is a large single stone hillock called Ballagerebetta which is 2975 ft above sea-level. Being located 2893 ft above mean sea level, K.G.F enjoys an equable climate same as that of Bangalore and is close to the boundaries of Tamil Nadu and Andhra Pradesh. Just before the advent of British mining companies on the field, the entire land was covered with irregular forest vegetations and posed an unattractive look. But, these unattractive features attracted the men of zeal who reached the peaks of suc- cess through hard work and perseverance. Result—on the once waste and

discarded land came a world famous Gold-mining industry and Gold town with Golden hearted citizens who created a Golden History!

CHAPTER THREE

ALL GLITTERS ARE NOT GOLD

Gold is the most dazzling and attracting thing in the universe; it was the first metal man ever recognized even before iron! It's a noble substance on our planet as also a dangerous metal for it spoils the mind of man. Its attractive colour, lustre, bright- ness, weight, resistance to corrosion and rarity of dense occurrence all put together make magical effects on human mind. The colour of gold cannot be imitated by any other metal or mixture of metals in the universe. Also, its beauty cannot be fully expressed even through the words of poets. These attracting properties of gold have pulled the attention of man since the Stone Age and he has developed curious fancy for it since then. Xenophanes, the Greek historian (350 BC) has noted: "The history of Grecian Goldmines goes into antiquity of unknown period." This indicates that, the king and queen of all metals in the universe has

accompanied human beings since the time they were cave-men. Because of these facts, gold always occupies great position in human history. Many other valuable substances are fancifully compared to gold; as, black gold, green gold, white gold or liquid gold; but, it's only the metal gold that is true gold. Also, it's only the field that bears gold is a Goldfield; but, not others.

CHAPTER FOUR

IMPACTS OF GOLD IN SEVERAL SPHERES!

Gold is a multifaceted metal because of its unique nature. It's a beautiful, lovely, Godly as also a dangerous metal. This magical metal unites and divides castes, religions, creeds, languages and rich and poor in societies. Over the ages, gold has so attracted man that it breaches all these social barriers. Are there anybody in India who could refuse accepting Gold when offered by a person at the lowest stra- tum of the society? No, and never could it be! In individual's life possessing gold signifies many things. Whether elites, middle class or the poor,—everyone wants to acquire and amass their wealth in the form of gold. In the poor man's mind,

gold instills a kind of confidence about their future; for a rich, it is their status sym- bol. Gold is also a dangerous metal both for the possessors and non-possessors. Those who possess it attracts dangers from thieves. Rarely, those who do not pos- sess it become so dangerous, for it spoils their mind and make them acquire or grab it by any means, thus make them indulge in unlawful activities! It is also dan- gerous for thieves since they can not hold it for long for fear of arrests. Gold is responsible for many of the changes in societies,—good and bad. Poss- ession of gold has always been the reason for misery, strife and double dealing even by some gentlemen and women. Many empires were defeated, crores of men were killed, new lands were discovered and new inventions were made in science. But it's sure, the fault for all these changes lies not in the metal but, in the mind. Sappho has noted: "Without the love of virtue, Gold is a dangerous and harmful guest among men." Gold also make man a fool! In his greediness man mistakes Pyrite,—a sulphide mixed Copper/Iron ore associated with gold bearing rocks as

gold ore. This ore, because of its deceptive golden appearance is cheating man since the time gold was discovered. Hence pyrite is called Fool's Gold and those attracted by it are called on the same line. Because of the noble properties of gold, Alchemists of middle ages aimed at converting base metals to gold; the result was many an advancements in chemistry.

CHAPTER FIVE

GOLDEN FLEECE

Not only man, but also heavenly beings (if any) as believed in several mythology also were greedy of gold! The famous legend of 'Golden Fleece' in Greek mythol- ogy is interesting. It was centered on an expedition to seize gold washed out of river sands with the aid of sheep-skin in the region now known as Armenia (erst- while state of Soviet Union). Animal skins with lengthy hairs were in use long ago in capturing gold from crushed ore in wet condition. It was believed, Phrixus and Helle the mythic characters flew with large quantity of gold on 'A flight of Golden Blanket' and disappeared into sky.

CHAPTER SIX

ALL THAT HE TOUCHED TURN TO GOLD

The present Lydia (Turkey) in ancient times was a good source of gold. River Pactolus was said to have enriched that land with a large wealth of Gold. A famous fable tells us: God Dionysus rewarded King Midas of his prayer that, all that he touched to become gold. Midas happily tested the boon; but instantly realized, it was altogether 'an inconvenient trophy'. The uneasiness caused by this 'self-cursed gift' drove the king to again pray for relief which he again obtained by bathing in Pactolus; thereupon, its sands became highly auriferous or 'Goldish'.

CHAPTER SEVEN

EL DORADO (THE MYTHIC GOLDEN LAND AND MAN)

So courageous, so adventurous, so ruthless and too foolish diehards they were! The strangest of all the strange approaches in man's attempt to discover Goldfields was 'El Dorado'. This non-existing Goldfield/man for several centuries have at- tracted many foolish, but courageous adventurers only to prove their misfortunes;

some of them lost their wealth and many their health! On their return adventures, several heroes also lost their already acquired reputations and attained 'fooldom'. All of them were losers. Many such heroes were relieved from the troubles of the world! Still, the craze on El Dorado created many dauntless adventurers. Some of the South American farm workers working in a cave shouted "El Do- rado, El Dorado"; they discovered El Dorado (?)—A Golden king was standing with his body guards on a golden raft; but it was all a golden model retrieved from sand! In 1538, an Indian narrated a story to a Spanish adventurer Sebastian de Belalcazar who conquered the Inca tribes on his mission to loot their gold. The narrator said: A tribal king sprinkled his body with gold powder and swam in Guatavita Lake. Belalcazar coined the name 'El Dorado'—meaning, a Golden man to the tribal king in narration. For centuries, El Dorado was thought to be a true Golden-man! This term has mesmerized the minds of men seeking gold for many centuries.

Gonzalo Jimenez de Quesada,—a Spaniard in 1540 set on his adventure in search of the mythic Eldorado with 1000 courageous men from Santa Maria of Colombia. Their voyage was so perilous that, they had to face the attacks by the pi- rates and suffer sea sickness etc. 800 of them attained eternity before they reached Chibehas. Their team now was reduced to just 200. At this stage, a humbug Indian took them to a lake which was just a water filled crater of an extinct volcano situ- ated at an altitude of 8800 feet. Alas! Nowhere could they see any Golden gentle man or a Golden Land. They returned home sadly and safely. Nearly 30 years after the above voyage, 'The Old Tiger'—none other than the same uncle Gonzalo planned to become young. He restarted his adventure with 3000 brave cum foolish sailors with the same aim of searching El Dorado! After a voyage of three years and tireless search, they were enlightened and decided not to undertake any such foolish adventures. They also became advisors to similar grow- ing heroes and advised them not to waste money, time, energy and lives.

After Gonzalo attained enlightenment, another learned old gentleman Antonio de Berrio,—the Governor of a territory near Amazon river wanted to prove he was young. He could have done it in a direct way; but followed the paths of his fore- runner Gonzalo. Antonio started his golden pilgrimage from central Colombia. He strongly believed that El Dorado was hiding somewhere in Guyana. Not to lose heart, he made two exemplary voyages in three years along with his follower gullibles. Within three years after the above voyage, the Governor gentleman started his third venture in a different direction to Trinidad Island. There, Antonio met another beautiful venturer Sir Walter Raleigh,—the Grand Ambassador of Her Imperial Majesty, Queen Elizabeth the Empress. Both the adventurers discussed a lot the entire night and Walter Raleigh hurriedly wrote a book on the experiences of Anto- nio without ascertaining the truth. These learned men too couldn't find out their 'hiding El Dorado'. Raleigh has mentioned in his writing the name 'Parima Lake'

Gonzalo Jimenez de Quesada,—a Spaniard in 1540 set on his adventure in search of the mythic Eldorado with 1000 courageous men from Santa Maria of Colombia. Their voyage was so perilous that, they had to face the attacks by the pirates and suffer sea sickness etc. 800 of them attained eternity before they reached Chibehas. Their team now was reduced to just 200. At this stage, a humbug Indian took them to a lake which was just a water filled crater of an extinct volcano situated at an altitude of 8800 feet. Alas! Nowhere could they see any Golden gentle man or a Golden Land. They returned home sadly and safely.

Nearly 30 years after the above voyage, 'The Old Tiger'—none other than the same uncle Gonzalo planned to become young. He restarted his adventure with 3000 brave cum foolish sailors with the same aim of searching El Dorado! After a voyage of three years and tireless search, they were enlightened and decided not to undertake any such foolish adventures. They also became advisors to similar growing heroes and advised them not to waste money, time, energy and lives.

After Gonzalo attained enlightenment, another learned old gentleman Antonio de Berrio,—the Governor of a territory near Amazon river wanted to prove he was young. He could have done it in a direct way; but followed the paths of his fore-runner Gonzalo. Antonio started his golden pilgrimage from central Colombia. He strongly believed that El Dorado was hiding somewhere in Guyana. Not to lose heart, he made two exemplary voyages in three years along with his follower gullibles.

Within three years after the above voyage, the Governor gentleman started his third venture in a different direction to Trinidad Island. There, Antonio met another beautiful venturer Sir Walter Raleigh,—the Grand Ambassador of Her Imperial Majesty, Queen Elizabeth the Empress. Both the adventurers discussed a lot the entire night and Walter Raleigh hurriedly wrote a book on the experiences of Antonio without ascertaining the truth. These learned men too couldn't find out their 'hiding El Dorado'. Raleigh has mentioned in his writing the name 'Parima Lake'

said to contain gold. His followers have seen and enjoyed El Dorado hundreds of times; but, in dreams! Even 200 years after his death, many greedy men tried to discover Parima, but in vain. El Dorado attracted one more wonderful expedition by a team led by Diez de la Fuente again a Spanish man. They sailed deep into Venezuela in search of Parima Lake only to decide not to proceed any further on imaginary matters! Diehard al- ways exists. A British Company during 19th century installed huge pumping machinery to pump out the entire waters of Guatavita Lake. They spent enormous sums on this project; but who could drink out the ocean? As in any other common lakes, these Britons could retrieve alluvial sands that contained traces of gold;—a century tragedy in search of gold ended for the time being!

CHAPTER EIGHT

PROPERTIES OF GOLD

The scientific name of Gold is 'Aurum' which means 'Glowing Dawn' and its

chemical symbol is Au. Aurum is derived from the Latin word Aurora,—meaning Sun God. Rocks that contain gold are called auriferous rocks. Gold is an inert ele- ment and an efficient conductor of electricity. It has an attractive lustre and colour and has got exceptionally heavy weight with a specific gravity of 19.3. Gold melts at 1063°C and boils at 2970°C temperatures. It is resistant to oxidizing and other common corrosive agents. It is un-tarnishable and remains bright at all temper- atures. Gold is insoluble in many of the common chemical agents; but in hot Selenic or Telluric acid. Aquaregia or 'The Royal Water' is a mixture of Nitric acid and Hydrochloric acid in 1:3 ratio which is the usual solvent that dissolves gold and platinum. Gold also dissolves in aqueous solutions of Potassium or Sodium Cyanide. It also dissolves in Sodium polysulfide. Gold is a highly malleable metal and can be shaped to any form we like by ham- mering. It can be beaten into a thin leaf of 0.0001mm or even less than a micron in thickness. One gram of gold can be made to cover an area of 5600 sq.cms (with a

thickness of 10000 part of a millimeter) Gold can be made into extremely thin foil. Egyptian tombs built during Stone Age have such foils in them. Gold foils are used as optical filters and for decorative purposes. Such foils are covered over glass and when invisible infra-red radiations are passed through it, a faint green colour is transmitted. Gold is so ductile, that one gram of it can be drawn into a wire of 2300 metres length. Purity of gold is expressed by the term 'Fine'. Fineness means, the number of parts gold make with a total of 1000 parts of metal mixture. Pure gold is 100% gold and its fineness is 1000. One carat of gold means one part of gold in 24 parts of the total metal and hence 24 carat gold is 1000 fine Gold rarely occur in chemical combination with other elements. Absolutely pure gold is not found in native state. Silver, Copper, Bismuth, Tungsten and Mercury are generally found in association with gold. When silver proportion with gold exceeds 20%, the alloy is called Electrum. Alloy of gold and copper is called Tumbaga. Gold extracted from the fields of K.G.F and Hutti mines has a fineness ranging from 875 to 920 and are the finest in India. Gold of Chigargunta mine has a fineness of 800.

CHAPTER NINE

IMPORTANCE OF GOLD

uring initial ages gold was used only for ornamental purposes, but at later times it was considered a repository of wealth. Such repositories of gold are found in the pyramids of Egypt from the time of Pharaoh Menes (3400 BC). Probably, it was from his time gold was being used as a medium of exchange in trade. The stability and value of gold was recognized by the commercial world only after a thousand years from the time of Pharaoh Menes. Gold commands high positions in all the countries for many reasons. It is a store of huge wealth in smallest spaces! It is used in settling-down trade affairs among different nations. It is used in direct monetary dealings, in making ornaments, in industries for gold plating (Rolled Gold) and in making thin films for use

in the laboratories. Gold is also used in dentistry, Ayurvedhic and Unani medicines. Jewellery gold is usually alloyed with Copper, Silver, Nickel and Palla- dium. In A.D 1717 'A Gold Standard' was set-in for business purposes. This standard was in partial practice during earlier times, but fully from 1821 and was common throughout the world. Gold coins (with guaranteed purity and weight) of fixed val- ues were minted and currency values were directly linked to it. This facilitated con- version between one or more currencies of different countries. The price of Sterling Pound of 3.89 per troy ounce of gold was fixed by the famous scientist Sir Isaac Newton in the year 1717 when he was the mint master at London. (1Troy ounce = 31.10428 gms of fine gold) Strangely the price fixed by Newton remained un- changed for about 200 years. Several factors and business ramifications in the in- ternational trade caused a tilt in this balance and the 'Gold Standard' was aban- doned in 1931. Gold also acts as one of the 'backings' in minting of currencies. For

this reason much of gold is kept as 'Bullion in Reserve' for the total value of notes issued. Between 1934-68, the American price of $35 per ounce of gold was in practice. This was equivalent to around £4.2 which in India at that time was Rs. 56 per ounce; that is to say, it was Rs. 1.80 per gram. The price of gold from 1968 is reaching sky- high and has become the 'wealth in dream' to poor people. Even though gold stan- dard was abolished officially, it continues to rule unofficially and is acceptable widely as a medium of exchange. Despite limited holdings of gold reserves, several countries continue to issue Gold-Coins in fixed weight and purity. But, these coins are not intended for circu- lation in general business. The countries and names of their gold coins are:

S.Africa Krugerrand
U.K Britannia
U.S. A Eagle
Canada Maple leaf
Australia Nugget
Austria Philharmonic Orchestra
China Panda

Belgium Ecu

Mexico Centenario

Cuba called by various names

Iran called by various names.

The monetary role of gold is gone; it now is a powerful market commodity and is a store of wealth at all levels of societies. Gold in the U.S Underground Vault: Gold mined from undergrounds goes again

to underground for being stored safely. The U.S has acquired gold worth 20000 million dollars (570 million ounces) which was more than half of the world's total supply of monetary gold. Out of this quantum, around 8000 tonnes of gold was the pledged properties of other poor countries. This fabulous treasure is neatly stacked in the under-ground vaults. This vault in Fort-Knox is a highly secured two level granite-steel & concrete sub-terranean room. It has an air-tight and water-tight interior with a 20 tonne stainless steel door. The location of this structure is sun-light proof and is fenced with a mesh charged with 5000 volts of electricity. Its outer tier has poisonous gases and heavy forceful water jets. There are 10 watch towers to guard this unit which are provided with Radio-technology and Automatic Monitor Systems. The guards on duty with ma- chineguns maintain round-the-clock vigil on the vault. These guards were ap- pointed after going through tough selection procedures. They themselves were put into strict monitoring. Also, the entire unit is provided with Electronic Surveillance

& Monitoring System. It is believed that, the erstwhile Soviet Union has deposited a large quantum of gold bars with the Federal Reserve Bank, 80 feet under Wall Street, New York.

CHAPTER TEN

DISCOVERY AND PRODUCTION OF GOLD IN MODERN TIMES

Gold during ancient times was mined from various parts of different countries. Many of those mines were closed prematurely for unknown reasons and were re- discovered in the modern times. Christopher Columbus set sailed from Spain in A.D 1492 on a mission to discover sea route to India. The voyagers on his flotil- la,—Santa Maria, Nina and Pinta were no madmen to discover a route just for trad- ing in spices, peacocks and monkeys; but the aim of Isabella was Gold. Columbus landed on a wrong (but right) destination. On his landing, the first words he ut- tered to the natives of Bahamas Island were: "Where is Gold?" The Spaniards in- dulged in ruthless killing of the natives on the new continent America, for

Columbus himself was tyrannical and merciless. So greedy for gold the Spaniards were; they crossed continents and oceans aim- ing on the magical metal. They were ready to risk any kind of adventures and to in- dulge in any kind of acts. In the 16th century, bearded and fair skinned Spaniards on horses' and mules' back with spears and other dreaded weapons conquered the Inca tribes of Peru in South America. The aim of Spaniards was looting the tombs of the dead for treasures. Firstly, they showered dazzling gifts to the local tribes for gold. If it failed, then they were sure to win the target with the supremacy of their arms and subdued the natives. Not only Spain, but also Dutch, Portugal and many other countries of the world aimed on the precious wealth of India as gold. Since the time gold was known to man, an estimated 80,000 tonnes has been ex- tracted throughout the world. In the modern times The North Carolina Goldfield of the United States was discovered in 1801. Gold was re-discovered in Kolar Gold Field in the year 1802, but, systematic mining was started in 1870s and success

met with in 1884. A gold deposit at Lena in Russia was discovered in 1829. The Goldfield at Georgia was discovered in 1829. The Mother-lode of California was discovered in 1847. Placer gold in California was discovered in 1848. In Australia gold was discovered in 1851 and in 1867 at Amur. In far-east maritime, gold was discovered in 1870s. The Emperor deposit at Fiji was discovered in 1872. S. African Goldmines were discovered in 1884 which were the largest and major producers in the world. In just a hundred years, it produced almost 40% of the total gold produced in the world in 6000 years. Since the time America was discovered by Christopher Columbus, South Amer- ica produced more than 80,00,000 ounces of gold or 35% of the world production between 1492 and 1600. A South-American mine in 17th century accounted for 61% and 80% in 18th century of world's output of gold. It produced around 4,80,00,000 ounces between 1700 and 1800. By 1853, U.S became the leading pro- ducer of gold in the world. With the discovery of Australian Goldfields in 1851, the

world's output was increased by 6million ounces between 1850 and 1860. This was followed by the discovery in western U.S; the Cripple Creek mine in Colorado in 1871 was a boost to the U.S. This development was surpassed by a S.African mine—'The Great Rand' in 1886. The discovery at Klondike in 1896 enhanced the world production of gold by 15 million ounces annually between 1890 and 1900. There was a peak production of 23 million ounces in 1915. S.Africa was the leading producer since 1905 which was seconded by the U.S until 1931 when Russia and Canada surpassed. Around 85% of the world's production of gold is being contributed by four major countries: S.Africa, United States, the former U.S.S.R and Canada. South Africa is the largest producer of gold in the world. It produced 700 tonnes in 1979 which was more than half of the world's production in that year. Soviets were also one of the largest producers. These two Republics were the major beneficiaries during any escalation of gold price. Thus, South African mining companies are the

richest in the world; but, their local mine labourers are living in poverty!

CHAPTER ELEVEN

THE WONDERFUL NUGGETS

Occurrence of gold in North America was in the form of dust or very fine grains; whereas, it was in the form of nuggets of large sizes in Australia. A large nugget called 'Holtermann Nugget' weighing 75Kgs was found in 1850s. Another gigantic nugget called 'The Welcome Stranger' was found in Victoria (Australia) in the year 1869; it weighed 2520 ounces. 'The Lady Hotham Nugget' weighed 1177 ounces and 'The Sierra Sands Nugget' (Africa) weighed 36,391 gms.

CHAPTER TWELVE

POSSESSION OF GOLD

In olden days, Europe obtained large quantities of gold from India through barter exchange and enriched its gold wealth. In India, around 8000 tonnes of gold are with private holdings as jewels. At the 1980s prevailed rate, its value was 1,12,000

crores. The cost of ten grams of gold in 1930s was Rs.17 (Rs.13 per 8 gms); in 1967 it was Rs.160/—and in 1980, it was Rs.1,700/—The cost of 8 gms of gold in 2011 exceeded Rs.22000/- United States of America is the largest holder of gold in the world. At the end of World War II, it held more than half of the total gold produced in the world. As on 31-12-1978, it possessed 276.4 million ounces. West Germany, the second largest holder held 118.6 million ounces and Britain 22.8 million ounces. The erstwhile Soviet Union, never disclosed such details; but it was believed, they held 45 million ounces.

Measurement

1grain = 64.80mgm

24grains = 1.55gms or 1penny weight (Pwt) or Dwt

1 Troy Ounce = 31.104gms or 20Dwt or 2.666

Tola

12Ounce (Ozs) = 1Pound 0r 373.25gms
1Kg = 32.15 Ozs or 2.68 Pounds
100Kg = 1 Quintal
10 Quintal = 1Metric Tonne or1000Kg
1Metric ton = 32,150 ounces
1Gm = 0.03215 Ozs

CHAPTER THIRTEEN

GOLD MINING DOWN THE AGES

(Adapted from an article 'Gold/Exploration and development'—A seminar vol.1985-United Nations Inter-regional Seminar on Gold.) An Out-line of the Chronology of Goldmining Worldwide Pre 4000 BC: Copper was in use in around 18000BC when gold too was

recognized along. During this period, metal working in copper and gold was start- ed in Balkan region of Europe. Lack of metallurgical knowledge of gold made the primitive men to just heap fine powder of native gold in caves simply to get excited at the attractive sight of the metal. It was in around 4000 BC that gold was actively sought for jewellery purposes. Oldest of such treasures of gold was found in Bul- garia in the year 1972 on the coast of Black-sea. Gold weighing about 5.5Kgs made into perfect pieces, 2000 in number were discovered there. There was also a dis- covery of two 6000 year old copper mines in Ai Bunar of Bulgaria and Rudna Glava of Yugoslavia. Upstream of rivers might have been their sources and panning was their extracting method. The way these pieces of gold were worked show the metal- lurgical knowledge of those ages. 4000-2000 BC: Placering was common in upper Egypt, Nubia (Sudan) and many other places. Mining for Quartz vein containing gold was in practice in Ethiopia where, extensive underground workings were recognized. Tunnels running

to around 6 Kms in length were also discovered in this region. Earlier men to some extent knew of the geology of their land. By 3500 BC, they dug shafts to a depth of 100 metres to follow the direction of the ore. Egyptians also have used tubular drilling with abrasive powder in their mining. The method of extraction of gold was by crushing and washing of the ore and they had knowledge of smelting. During this time, metallurgy was primitive. 2000-1000BC: Sutherland in 1960, Forbes in 1971, Boyle in 1979 and Mohide in 1981 have all noted: "Apart from Egypt and Transylvania, placers were also worked in Ireland, Mesopotamia and China. By 2000 BC, placers of Pactolus in Lydia (Tur- key) were discovered. Fire setting on rocks and quenching them with cold water was the method of breaking the ore in these regions. Due to primitive form of metallurgy, gold produced by Egyptians were whitish in colour because of inclu- sion of other impurities like silver, copper and platinum." A typical mining segment with a shaft, tunnels, a water well and workers' living

place was depicted in 1350 BC in 'Turin Papyrus',—the oldest map known to this day. Pure gold was obtained in around 1000 BC. During this period man learnt that, Gold adheres to mercury to form amalgam and was used in the process of gold separation. Another process called 'Liquation' was introduced in smelting. Im- pure gold ingots were obtained by smelting gold ore with silicious flux. These in- gots were alloyed with lead which was heated to a temperature between melting point of lead and copper. Lead would liquate out carrying with it silver and gold. Lead was then cupelled or refined to bone ash. Silver was separated using com- mon salt and pure gold was the result. The total gold produced during 2000- 1000BC was three times more than that of its previous production. King Solomon of 1000BC was getting a regular of 18 tonnes of gold per year from his subjugates. 1000 BC-700AD: Ancient historian Sagui has noted: "Man knew the importance of geological thinking and understood the fault displacements in the undergrounds during their search for gold in Cassandra of Greece." In 450 BC, Herodotus has

noted the relation of gold to quartz veining. He has written: "sheep skins with long hairs as liners were used in sluices to capture fine gold in Balkans, Russia etc." 753 BC marked the traditional founding of Rome and by the start of the modern era (1st millennium AD) Romans have mined around 30-40 tonnes of ore in the Spanish mines. They used Archimedes screws to dewater their mines. Diodorus in the 2nd century BC described the mining methods of his times. He has written, "Slaves were working in the underground mines with lamps strapped to their fore- heads and young boys carried the ore to surface." Pliny describes: "Gold produc- tion through first century AD dwindled in the Rome's Spanish mines which hith- erto were producing around 10 tonnes a year. The great deposits of Ireland, Egypt, Lydia and Georgian Russia were also fast depleting at the shallow depths or devel- oped at depths where mining was not practicable." A.D. 700-1500: By 8th century AD, Western countries could not produce any new gold, for they thought all their gold deposits were exhausted. World's attention

was slowly turned towards eastern countries for finding new store of gold. By now, the eastern countries also developed technology. In 13th century AD, Muslim al- chemists succeeded in separating gold from silver using

Nitric acid. 9th to 13th century AD marked the lowest production of gold in Europe; whereas, South Amer- ica, Asia, Africa, Inca and Aztec continued to mine gold by using old methods. They amassed large quantity of gold. The Incan ruler paid his ransom in gold to the Spaniard Pizzaro who conquered Peru in 1532. During 1522-1547, around 30 metric tonnes of gold was shifted from Mexico to Spain. In 1556, Agricola's famous book 'De Re Metallica' pulled the attention of the world in which history of gold, meth- ods and problems of mining and extraction methods are all explained. During 1492-1600, South America alone produced around 40% of world's pro- duction of gold at that time. This enormous production in the next 300 years in the great placers of Brazil and Colombia resulted in huge wealth that triggered the Re- naissance and the Industrial Revolution in Europe. Industrial Revolution allowed

gold production in the 19th and 20th century on a large scale undreamt of even in the olden times. A.D. 1600-1850: South American mines were all confined to shallow depths. (During A.D. 700 and1500 the world production of gold was 2 metric tonnes a year. This production rose to around 9 metric tonnes a year in the 16th century). S.African mines produced 15 tonnes a year in the 18th century. 19th century saw the major discoveries in the Ural Mountains and Oxus valley in Russia. Chlorination method was introduced in 18th century and cyanidation in later part of 19th cen- tury. Chlorine gas was passed through wet crushed ore, the resultant gold chloride is then separated using water and precipitated with ferrous sulphate. South Amer- ican fields yield large quantity of gold. This resulted in the migration of people from Europe to S.America during 17, 18 and 19th centuries. The gold so extracted there all went to France, England and Holland. During the early 19th century, the only notable Goldmine of N. America was Carolina's mine. At the 'free and easily

workable' Goldmine of California, Carolina's mine was deserted. A.D. 1850-1900: At the commencement of a Goldmine in California, a 'Gold Rush' was started between 1849 and 1850. Around 4,00,000 metal seekers rushed to that place to try their fortune. California Gold Rush was unique in the history of Goldmining of the world for many reasons. No government,—state or rulers of that region stake a claim over this Goldfield. Any-body fit enough to compete the 'Rush' could mine any quantum of gold and keep it for them. California Gold Rush also created such rushes on many places. Knowledge on panning of sediments, prospecting and identifying of gravels led to the discovery of 'The Great Comstock Lode' in Nevada in 1859. Features com- mon between California and Australia led to the discovery of Gold at New South Wales in1951. What was staked by two gold prospectors Moses and Fred Manuel later became the world famous 'Homestake Gold' in S.Dakota. This field is the largest producer of gold in the western hemisphere; Carolina's mines of Nevada in

U.S ranks second. The result was that, the world's production of gold jumped eight-fold from 24 tonnes between 1800-1850 to 200 tonnes a year from 1851-1900. Technology and new ideas added boost to 'Gold Explosion'. Steel and explosives were used, mines were dewatered by pumps and stone mortars were replaced with stamp mills. Electric power brought in dramatic and un-imaginable changes in mining. Diamond drills were introduced in drilling in 1862. In 1867, steam driven mills were introduced. In 1871, steam driven pumps came to use. Cyanidation suc- cessfully produced expected results in which recovery of gold touched 99.5% from 70%.

Technology opened up new areas in mining which made possible the hither- to considered impossible; difficult metallurgical processes were made simple. K.G.F mines was started during 1870s at a time when many scientific innovations made their entry into human life. 1900 and onwards: Sophisticated approaches are being made in mining owing to the engineering advances in 19th, 20th and 21st centuries. There has been steady progress in all the disciplines concerning mining and metallurgy. Geo-physical prospecting both on ground and from satellites has been so helpful in bringing out results. Electricity is the most overwhelming force that takes the mining to further depths (progress) and enables efficient functioning. Owing to stable price and in- crease in cost of mining, world production decreased in 1950s and 60s.

CHAPTER FOURTEEN

PLACER DEPOSITS

Gold is recovered from earth since time immemorial both on surface and under- grounds. It is a widely distributed metal but occurs in less abundance. Metal de- posits formed due to mechanical concentration along the flow courses of rivers are called Placers or secondary deposits. Around 22% of the world production of gold are obtained from secondary deposits. For many millennia, river alluvium was the chief source of gold production throughout the world. Placers are fine gravels which contain residue of metallic contents. They are driven to different places through natural transport agents like streams and rivers which flow on

metalliferous tracts of rocks. These agents erode the surface and carry the sedi- ments across the courses of their flow. The metal contents in them due to their weights settle down the bottom and on accumulation remain deposited in the bed along with other sediments. Gold, due to its high density and chemical inertness are found unmixed with other metals as placer deposits. These particles of gold occur in two forms—solid and fine powder. The solid forms are called 'Nuggets' which vary in size from fraction of a millimeter to more than many inches. The nuggets grow in size on further concentration and become large. These lumps are called 'Native Gold' which remain embedded in depressions along the flow. In India large size of a nugget was found in Honnali taluk of Shimoga district in Kar- nataka in the year 1907; it weighed 4½ ozs.

CHAPTER FIFTEEN

OH, GOLDEN RIVERS!

Alluvium of most of the rivers in the world contains placer Gold. For this reason, many rivers in India were named after gold. Some of such popular names are: Swarnarekha, Swarnavathi, Honnuhole (Golden well), Ponnupuzha (Golden stream) Pennar or Ponnaaru (Golden river) Ponnamaravathy, Ponni or Ponneer- Cauvery (Golden water), Ponn-parappi (that which spreads gold) Ponnani (Golden jewel) and Ponneri (Golden lake). Sea water contains 5 to 250 parts of gold per thousand million parts of water; that is to say, the concentration of gold in sea water is only .000006 parts per 10,00,000 parts of water. Attempts to profitably re- cover gold from this source failed. In India, enormous quantity of gold was recovered by placering even until the

start of 19th century. From this time native methods gave way for modern under- ground mining and thus came the large Goldmining industry,—the Kolar Gold Field!

CHAPTER SIXTEEN

LODE DEPOSITS

When placer deposits were exhausted to the means of primitive methods, man's attention was shifted towards vein or lode type of gold deposits. The ancient metal seekers have fully exploited the openly visible rich gold ores on surfaces leaving only the under-grounds. Vein types are directly associated with the rocks. Unlike the placer form, gold occur in large rock masses as veins and reefs called lodes. Recovery from underground lodes requires sophisticated scientific approaches which again demand technology, finance and human determination. The last one is the foremost requisite in all under ground type of mining. In India, we have stories of both surface and underground types of mining for

size of a nugget was found in Honnali taluk of Shimoga district in Karnataka in the year 1907; it weighed 4½ ozs.

Oh, Golden Rivers!

Alluvium of most of the rivers in the world contains placer Gold. For this reason, many rivers in India were named after gold. Some of such popular names are: Swarnarekha, Swarnavathi, Honnuhole (Golden well), Ponnupuzha (Golden stream) Pennar or Ponnaaru (Golden river) Ponnamaravathy, Ponni or Ponneer-Cauvery (Golden water), Ponn-parappi (that which spreads gold)

Ponnani (Golden jewel) and Ponneri (Golden lake). Sea water contains 5 to 250 parts of gold per thousand million parts of water; that is to say, the concentration of gold in sea water is only .000006 parts per 10,00,000 parts of water. Attempts to profitably recover gold from this source failed.

In India, enormous quantity of gold was recovered by placering even until the

start of 19th century. From this time native methods gave way for modern underground mining and thus came the large Goldmining industry,—the Kolar Gold Field!

Lode Deposits (Gold from on and underground rocks)

When placer deposits were exhausted to the means of primitive methods, man's attention was shifted towards vein or lode type of gold deposits. The ancient metal seekers have fully exploited the openly visible rich gold ores on surfaces leaving only the under-grounds. Vein types are directly associated with the rocks. Unlike the placer form, gold occur in large rock masses as veins and reefs called lodes. Recovery from underground lodes requires sophisticated scientific approaches which again demand technology, finance and human determination. The last one is the foremost requisite in all under ground type of mining.

In India, we have stories of both surface and underground types of mining for

gold. Whilst placer deposit recovery is universal, underground type of mining are confined to places where there are rich deposits in rocks. We have several evidences to establish that, underground mining for gold was very active since an- cient times. Such ancient mining were extensive and widespread in India partic- ularly in South or the Deccan. The earliest men exploited the gold bearing fields to their fullest ability and capacity at their disposal.

They finally discarded them at a stage when they were not able to cope up with the natural problems. Such dis- carded fields remained untouched for more than a thousand years until the early 19th century when some British enterprises commenced operating these fields. In their endeavour, they met with full success only in Kolar Gold Fields. To some ex- tent, the Hutti Gold Field of Raichur district in Karnataka and later, the Ramagiri Gold Field of Andhra Pradesh were also yielding some profit for the modern min- ers. During the early years of modern Goldmining, the ores of K.G.F mines assayed

more than 45 gms per tonne, which in course of time came down to 6-8 gms. (At one stage it was 160 gms/ tonne!) Ores of Ramagiri mines assayed 4-5gms per tonne; whereas, the average grade of ore of Wayanaad Gold Fields of Kerala was 2-3 gms per tonne. While all the other minor fields in India met their tragedy, it was only the K.G.F mines that could be worked out for more than a century without a break. It's there- fore said that, the Golden age of Goldmining industry in India dawned on K.G.F in 1880, but was made to end in 2001 in the same city after creating a Golden history.

CHAPTER SEVENTEEN

SYNTHESIS OF GOLD BU ALCHEMY

Is it practicable to synthesize gold by artificial methods? Ancient Indian scientists were believed to have synthesized gold by the process of alchemy. In this method, elements of the nearest atomic weights to gold were said to be converted to gold by employing Siddha and Ayurvedic methods! They were also believed to have pro- duced gold by mixing juices of certain herbs that contain gold. Using techniques not known to others, the ancient Indian scientists (Rishis or Sages) were said to have isolated gold from plant bodies for medicinal purposes. Muslim alchemists of Middle East also attempted to produce artificial gold. Whether they succeeded in their attempts or not, a great deal of advancements in chemistry was achieved dur- ing their researches!

CHAPTER EIGHTEEN

THE FIRST MODERN GOLD MINING IN INDIA

n 1792, a commission constituted by the British has recorded: "The Rajah of Nil- ambur (Wayanaad) claimed royalty on gold won on his territory, but no active steps were taken to develop this gold industry." In around 1865, Mr. J.W. Minchen erected mining machinery to crush the quartz extracted from the Skull reef which later became the famous Alpha Gold Mine in Kerala. It is believed, this might be the foundation for a modern Goldmining industry in India. By 1880, the occurrence of a large lode was discovered at Kolar Gold Field and active mining industry was established. Encouraged by the discovery, Mr.R.Bruce Foote of Geological Survey of India submitted a report on several auriferous tracts of old Mysore (Karnataka) state in 1886 and 1887. By 1898, 67 mining blocks were formed in Karnataka excluding K.G.F and its vicinity. Around 20 companies or syndicates and individuals operated these fields. Though many of them worked with determinations, none of them could meet success. Until1914, the total gold produced out side K.G.F. was only 1000 ounces and all operations by then came to end.

CHAPTER NINETEEN

GOLD MINES OF INDIA

The following were the chief Goldfields of India:

1. Kolar Gold Fields of Kolar district in Karnataka,
2. Hutti Gold Fields of Raichur district in Karnataka,
3. Gadag Gold Fields of Dharwad district in Karnataka,
4. Wayanaad Gold Fields of Kerala (formerly Nilgiris dist) and
5. Ramagiri Gold Fields of Ananthpur district of Andhra Pradesh.

Other smaller Goldfields which were active for some times were:

1. Bisnattam of Chittoor district of A.P. (adjoining southern border of K.G.F) and
2. Gooty in Ananthpur district of A.P.

Goldfields of minor importance (Karnataka),—prospected and subsequently aban- doned were in:

1. Bellara—Tumkur district,
2. Ajjanhalli—Tumkur district,
3. Lakkavalli—Chikmagalur district,
4. Jalagargundi—Chikmagalur district,
5. Kempinkote—Hassan district,

6. Honnali-Shimoga district,
7. Honnehatti—Shimoga district,
8. Kudurekonda and palavanahalli—Shimoga district,
9. Hadabanatta, Kowdali and Bensibetta-Mysore district and adjacent parts of Coimbatore district,
10. Kabligatti—Dharwad district,
11. Manglur-Gulbarga district.

Other auriferous veins of not much economic value are found in many parts of Karnataka, adjacent parts of Tamil Nadu and Andhra Pradesh; majority of them

were abandoned. In Wayanaad, alluvial gold has been worked since ancient times. Following a favourable report on that field in 1878 by Mr King of Geological Survey of India, around 33 companies were floated in England. Within 4-5 years most of these mines were closed as the value of ore extracted were poor and 3-4 companies managed to stay till the end of 19th century. Many important mining companies also operated other fields with a capital of over half a million pounds. They were: The Kempinkote Goldmine Co., in Hassan dist. The Ajjanahalli mining prospects in Chitaldurg dist. The Bellara mine, The Amble and Woolagiri mines in Nanjangud dist. The Jalagargundi mines in Shimoga dist. and Honnali and Palavanahalli Goldmines Company. None of these mines ever paid dividends or returned any capital to its shareholders. The Department of Mines and Geology of the Government of Mysore operated the Bellara mines at Chitaldurg and 2000 ounces of gold from 20000 tons of ore was obtained. These operations proved uneconomical and were ceased in 1954. Some of the companies

of K.G.F also invested on these option blocks of other area mines. Following the works of Brucefoote, Mr.Hughes-Hughes of G.S.I discovered gold bearing reefs in the Maski schist band of Hyderabad state. A company called Hyderabad (Deccan) Company obtained mineral rights to mine this area. Between 1887 and 1889, this company discovered three hundred different gold occurrences in Raichur dist. but, only few of the ancient works discovered were prospected. This company, together with Wondalli (Deccan) Gold Mining Company Ltd. spent over £4,00,000 in prospecting and mine development. Here, the Boodinnie mine was worked in 1883, but gold worth £8700 was extracted on spending £36000 and hence all works were suspended. Another failure was the Kadoni mine located around 4 miles from Wondalli village was closed in 1898. Wondalli mine near the present Hutti mine went deep by 750 feet and its out put was only 15000 ounces. This company also failed and was liquidated in 1901 with no dividends paid to its share holders.

Hutti Gold Field was prospected during 1903-20 and was abandoned. It was later re-opened and prospected on a moderate scale. The Hyderabad (Deccan) Mining Company which fared so disastrously was abandoned. But, it was only the remain- ing faith in one of its officers that carried the work untiringly which later estab- lished the famous Hutti Company in 1901. Hutti was the deepest ancient mine in the world which has a depth of 640 feet below the ground. This mine has pro- duced 237000 ounces of gold from 417000 tonnes of ore milled. This mine was closed in 1921 as it was believed that, the ore was exhausted, but was reopened later. Due to modern mining, Hutti reached a total depth of 300 metres. Topuldodi Gold Mines near Hutti produced 2132 ounces of gold worth approx- imately £9000 and was closed after three years of operations; burying with it was a capital of £90000 in 1921. The Ooregum Company and Deccan Gold Field Corpo- ration worked the

Manglur mine, Brahmins' well and Maski No.7 prospect; but unrewarding results made them wind up their operations in 1914. Probably, a total

of K.G.F also invested on these option blocks of other area mines.

Following the works of Brucefoote, Mr.Hughes-Hughes of G.S.I discovered gold bearing reefs in the Maski schist band of Hyderabad state. A company called Hyderabad (Deccan) Company obtained mineral rights to mine this area. Between 1887 and 1889, this company discovered three hundred different gold occurrences in Raichur dist. but, only few of the ancient works discovered were prospected. This company, together with Wondalli (Deccan) Gold Mining Company Ltd. spent over £4,00,000 in prospecting and mine development. Here, the Boodinnie mine was worked in 1883, but gold worth £8700 was extracted on spending £36000 and hence all works were suspended. Another failure was the Kadoni mine located around 4 miles from Wondalli village was closed in 1898. Wondalli mine near the present Hutti mine went deep by 750 feet and its out put was only 15000 ounces. This company also failed and was liquidated in 1901 with no dividends paid to its share holders.

Hutti Gold Field was prospected during 1903-20 and was abandoned. It was later re-opened and prospected on a moderate scale. The Hyderabad (Deccan) Mining Company which fared so disastrously was abandoned. But, it was only the remaining faith in one of its officers that carried the work untiringly which later established the famous Hutti Company in 1901. Hutti was the deepest ancient mine in the world which has a depth of 640 feet below the ground. This mine has produced 237000 ounces of gold from 417000 tonnes of ore milled. This mine was closed in 1921 as it was believed that, the ore was exhausted, but was reopened later. Due to modern mining, Hutti reached a total depth of 300 metres.

Topuldodi Gold Mines near Hutti produced 2132 ounces of gold worth approximately £9000 and was closed after three years of operations; burying with it was a capital of £90000 in 1921. The Ooregum Company and Deccan Gold Field Corporation worked the Manglur mine, Brahmins' well and Maski No.7 prospect; but unrewarding results made them wind up their operations in 1914. Probably, a total

capital of £500000 was lost in the unsuccessful mining in Hyderabad regions alone. In 1842, the presence of alluvial gold in Dharwar district was first reported; but in 1874, Bruce Foote recognized numerous ancient mine pits there. It is recorded that, an Australian miner in 1861 prospected these areas on behalf of the govern- ment. Later, he formed a company in Bombay (Mumbai) to work alluvial gold in Satur area. He also sank many pits; but in 1866 he suddenly disappeared perhaps fearing for the shareholders to whom he was answerable about the failures. It was said that, he spent £15000 of the company but, no returns obtained excepting few nuggets of gold which he was sending from time to time to allay the fears of share- holders. But, again it was due to the efforts by Bruce Foote that prospectors were attracted in 1902. The Dharwar Gold Mines Ltd. was the first company formed to prospect this area which had a capital of £45000. It sold its mining leases to Dhar- war Reefs Ltd. at various periods and ceased in 1909. By 1907, at least 10 mining

companies were floated to operate a total of 50 blocks. The Dharwar Reefs Com- pany with a capital of £175000 worked some blocks and was the only company that operated a mill. This mine was developed to a depth of 1240 ft with a tunnel driv- ing of 32000 ft. By the time this mine was closed in 1911, it produced 14800 ounces of gold from 14171 tonnes of refractory ore (complex ore). Hosur Goldmines of Dharwar Ltd. was formed in 1907 with a capital of £250000. It reached a depth of 700ft with encouraging results, but was liquidated following failure of its Bankers. Sangli Gold Mines Ltd. was formed in the year 1902 with a capital of £75000. By the time it was reconstructed twice, it had spent a capital of £100000 and ceased operation in 1910. The Mysore Gold Mining Co. Ltd., the Champion Reef Gold Mines of India Ltd. and other companies of K.G.F also had option leases in Dharwar mines. These companies made a great deal of serious efforts and spent over £100000. The Mysore Company of K.G.F spent £27400 in three years and completed 2080ft of shaft sinking, 700 ft of winzing and rising and 7280ft of cross cutting. The Cham- pion Reef Company completed over 3500ft of shaft sinking, 800ft of winzes and 6800ft of tunneling in three years at a cost of £33000.

CHAPTER TWENTY

GREAT LOSS: UNFORTUNATE DHARWAR GOLD MINES

A total of £500000 was lost into the Dharwarian pits which deceived the mining companies. Though good value ores were found below the ancient workings, it didn't persist further below. The value of ores mined was not sufficient to produce profits. The companies also fell short of capital and hence, all works eventually came to halt in 1912. This company just produced not more than 16000 or 17000 ounces valued at £70000. The Anantpur Gold Mines in Andhra Pradesh was the last one to be started in

India in the year1905. The Anantpur Gold Field Ltd. The North Anantpur Gold Mines Ltd. and the Jibutil Gold Mines of Anantpur Ltd. were the leading companies that operated these areas. Conditions that arose during the First World War posed difficulties in raising additional capital and supply of equipments was also affected. This resulted in the closure of this mine, but was reopened later. The

Ramagiri Goldmines of Anantpur was also one of the mines that yield results.

CHAPTER TWENTY-ONE

BIHAR AND ODISHA

There are many places believed to contain Gold in Bihar, but their prospecting proved disappointing. Alluvial gold has been worked in Singhbhum, Manbhum and neighbouring areas, as also areas of former Bonai, Bamra, Gangpur and Jash- pur of Orissa. Kundrakocha of singhbhum district was worked for some time be- fore 1920. Ichagarh, Burudih and Maysare areas of Manbhum district were tried and no worthwhile quantities of gold produced. Some of the areas of Chotanagpur like Sonapet, Pahardih, and Lowa were also auriferous, but were of uneconomical

grade. Lowa is in the southern portion of Manbhum district. A firm known as Patkum Company was formed to prospect the surrounding areas of Lowa in 1891, but Lowa escaped attention. The old workings in Lowa Goldfield area comprised auriferous quartz occurrences in the hilly region called Bhaluk khad and Tamapahar. Since the days of pioneers likeV.Ball, W.King and R.Brucefoote in 1880s, Geolog- ical Survey of India is doing a tremendous investigation on modern lines to explore gold in many parts of India. Later workers like F.H.Hatch, H.H.Hayden and J.M.Maclaren have also contributed much to the investigation. We shall hope, G.S.I would do further lot towards establishing master Goldmines like that of Kolar Gold Fields. It is of interest to note that excluding Kolar Gold Fields and to some extent Hutti and Ramagiri mines, all other Goldmines in India were utter failures. More than £7

million (at the 19th century rate) was sunk into these Goldmines; but lost!

TO BE CONTINUED.....

Printed by Libri Plureos GmbH in Hamburg,
Germany